Ripley Readers

All true and unbelievable!

Learning to read. Reading to learn!

LEVEL ONE Sounding It Out Preschool–Kindergarten
For kids who know their alphabet and are starting to sound out words.

learning sight words • beginning reading • sounding out words

LEVEL TWO Reading with Help Preschool–Grade 1
For kids who know sight words and are learning to sound out new words.

expanding vocabulary • building confidence • sounding out bigger words

LEVEL THREE Independent Reading Grades 1–3
For kids who are beginning to read on their own.

introducing paragraphs • challenging vocabulary • reading for comprehension

LEVEL FOUR Chap
For confident readers w   d story.

reading for lea.   nt • feeding curiosity

Ripley Readers Designed to help kids build their reading skills and confidence at any level, this program offers a variety of fun, entertaining, and unbelievable topics to interest even the most reluctant readers. With stories and information that will spark their curiosity, each book will motivate them to start and keep reading.

PUBLISHING

Vice President, Licensing & Publishing   Amanda Joiner
Editorial Manager   Carrie Bolin

Editor   Jessica Firpi
Writer   Korynn Wible-Freels
Designer   Scott Swanson
Reprographics   Bob Prohaska
Production Design   Luis Fuentes

Published by Ripley Publishing 2021

10 9 8 7 6 5 4 3 2 1

Copyright © 2021 Ripley Publishing

ISBN: 978-1-60991-407-3

No part of this publication may be reproduced in whole or in part, stored in a retrieval system, or transmitted in any form by any means, electronic, mechanical, photocopying, recording, or otherwise, without written permission from the publisher.

For more information regarding permission, contact:
VP Licensing & Publishing
Ripley Entertainment Inc.
7576 Kingspointe Parkway, Suite 188
Orlando, Florida 32819

Email: publishing@ripleys.com
www.ripleys.com/books
Manufactured in China in May 2020.

First Printing

Library of Congress Control Number:
2020937129

PUBLISHER'S NOTE
While every effort has been made to verify the accuracy of the entries in this book, the Publisher cannot be held responsible for any errors contained in the work. They would be glad to receive any information from readers.

RIPLEY Readers

Odd Ocean!

All true and unbelievable!

RIPLEY
PUBLISHING

a Jim Pattison Company

Did you know that water covers most of the world?

Take a look at the ocean and you
will find some pretty weird things!

These pink and blue jellies sure know how to light up the water!

The glowing anglerfish lives
3,000 feet down where it is
cold and dark.

What makes this waterfall so amazing?

It is under water! You can see it best from up in the sky.

Sailors have been afraid of killer waves for hundreds of years. These big walls of water can come out of nowhere!

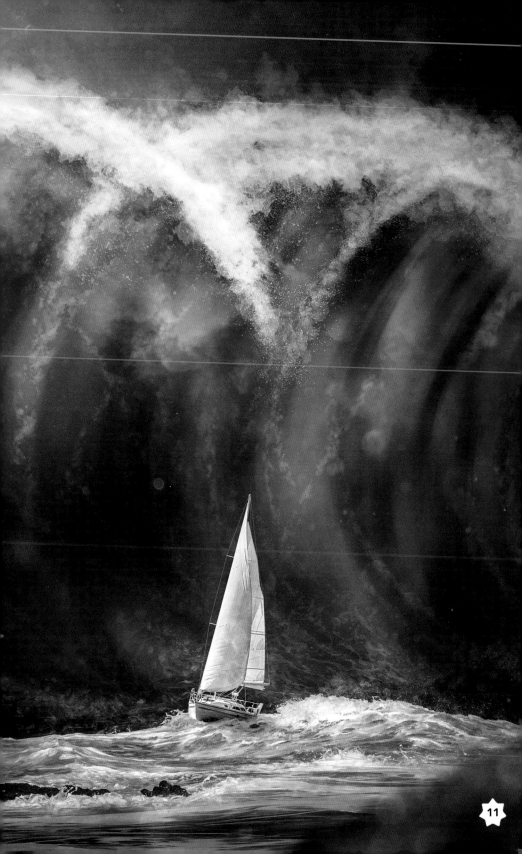

Did you know that an octopus has not one, not two, but *three* hearts?

They pump *blue* blood through the body and to the gills!

The mako shark is the fastest shark in the sea. Topping out at 42 miles an hour, the fish don't stand a chance!

You wouldn't want to be a fish swimming over a bobbit worm.

It shoots up from the ground and drags its food under the sand!

A fish out of water? The flying fish jumps above the ocean to escape its predators!

They can glide as far as 1,300 feet. That's farther than three soccer fields!

Why have spikes when you can just borrow them?

The boxer crab picks up anemones and swings them at fish!

This toothy monster has been around since the dinosaurs!

The lamprey's round mouth is full of sharp teeth. Yikes!

White humpback whales are very pretty and very rare!

This one's name is Migaloo. He was found off the coast of Australia.

Don't be fooled by this little guy's size. A mantis shrimp's punch can crack a crab shell and even a glass fish tank!

Did you know that sperm whales like to sleep up and down?

They look like big floating towers under the water! How funny is that?

A giant squid can grow almost as long as a city bus!

Not even half of the world's oceans have been explored. That means there are many more mysteries just waiting to be discovered!

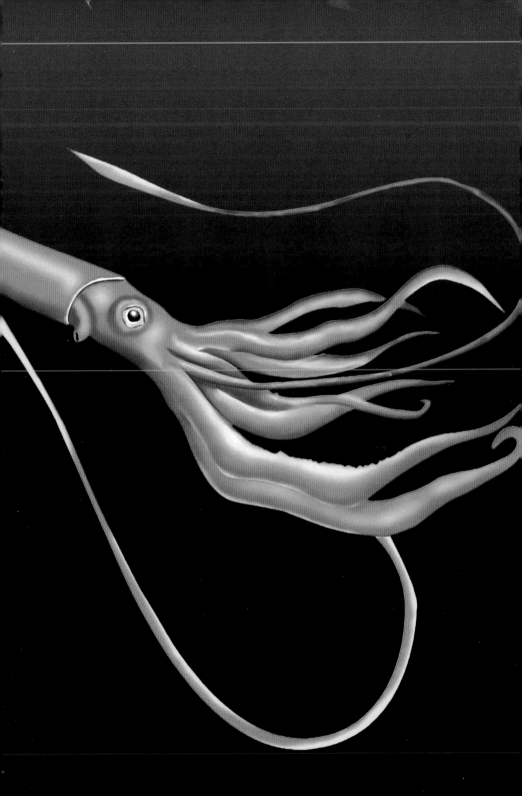

Ready for More?

Ripley Readers feature unbelievable
but true facts and stories!

LEVEL ONE
Sounding it out

LEVEL TWO
Reading with help

LEVEL THREE
Independent reading

LEVEL FOUR
Chapters

**For more information about
Ripley's Believe It or Not!, go to www.ripleys.com**